The RAMAYANA

IN PICTURES

ILLUSTRATIONS Jagdish Joshi
TEXT Mala Dayal

Rupa & Co

For Naina
with love

Published 2006 by
Rupa & Co
7/16, Ansari Road, Daryaganj
New Delhi 110 002

Sales Centres:
Allahabad Bangalore Chandigarh Chennai
Hyderabad Jaipur Kathmandu
Kolkata Mumbai Pune

Typeset & Layout by Arrt Creations
45 Nehru Apts, Kalkaji
New Delhi 110 019
arrt@vsnl.com

Printed in India by
Gopsons Paper Ltd
A-14 Sector 60
Noida 201 301

LONG, long ago, a good and kind King, Dasharath, ruled over the kingdom of Kosala. The beautiful city of Ayodhya was the capital of Kosala.

Dasharath had three queens — Kausalya, Sumitra and Kaikeyi.

King Dasharath had four sons:
the eldest was Ram, then Bharat,
and then the twins, Lakshman and
Shatrughan.

As the years went by, the four
princes learned the holy books and
the arts of war.

Ram grew into a brave and handsome young man. He was so strong that he broke the mighty bow of Lord Shiva which all the other princes had failed to do. Thus Ram won the hand of the beautiful princess Sita, daughter of Janak, the king of Mithila.

The people of Kosala and Mithila were filled with joy. There was
a grand wedding.

Many years passed…

One day, King Dasharath said to himself, "I am growing old. Ram is brave, kind and wise. I will make him Crown Prince. He will rule the country."

Everyone was very happy.

Only one person was not happy that Ram was to be Crown Prince.
That was Queen Kaikeyi's maid Manthara.

Manthara rushed to Queen Kaikeyi.

"Remember that a long time ago King Dasharath had promised to grant you two wishes. Tell the King to send Ram to the forest for fourteen years and make Bharat Crown Prince," said the wicked Manthara.

King Dasharath was very unhappy when he heard Queen Kaikeyi's two wishes. But a King has to keep his word. King Dasharath had promised Queen Kaikeyi that he would grant her two wishes.

9

When Ram was told he was being sent to the forest for fourteen years, he bowed his head. He agreed at once to do as his father wished.

The next day Ram left the palace with his wife Sita and brother Lakshman to live in the forest like a sadhu.

The people of Ayodhya wept to see them go.

Dasharath was so filled with sorrow when Ram left that he died of a broken heart.

When Bharat heard that Ram had been sent to the forest for fourteen years and that he was to be crowned King, Bharat was very angry with Queen Kaikeyi. "I love my brother Ram. I shall beg him to come back from the forest. Ram shall be King of Kosala."

Bharat set off with the army and Dasharat's three Queens to bring Ram back to Ayodhya.

Bharat fell at Ram's feet and begged him to come back to Ayodhya. But Ram refused. So Bharat took Ram's sandals, put them on the throne and ruled in Ram's name.

In the forest, among birds that sang joyfully and elephants and deer that roamed about happily, Lakshman built a hut. Ram, Sita and Lakshman lived there.

One day, Srupnakha, the sister of the Demon King of Lanka, Ravan, saw Ram and Lakshman. Ram was very handsome and Srupnakha fell in love with him. She asked Ram to marry her.

Ram said he was already married and told Srupnakha to ask Lakshman.
Srupnakha did not know that Ram was joking.

Srupnakha said, "You do not love me because you love Sita. I will eat
her up," and she rushed towards Sita.

Lakshman took out his sword and cut off Srupnakha's nose.

Srupnakha rushed to her brother Ravan and told him that Lakshman had cut off her nose.

Ravan was very angry. He thought of a clever plan to punish Ram and carry off the beautiful Sita.

One day when Sita was gathering flowers, she saw a beautiful golden deer with silver spots.

Sita wanted to have the deer as a pet. So Ram went after the deer leaving Lakshman to look after Sita. This was what Ravan had planned to get Ram away.

Ram chased the deer deep into the forest. Finally, he shot the deer with an arrow.

As the deer fell down, it changed into a demon and cried loudly, "Oh Sita! Oh Lakshman!" in a voice that sounded exactly like Ram's.

Sita thought Ram was hurt. She told Lakshman to go quickly and help Ram.

Lakshman did not want to leave Sita, but Sita begged him to go and help Ram. Finally Lakshman agreed.

Before leaving, Lakshman drew a magic circle around the hut. "Stay within this circle and you will be safe," Lakshman told Sita.

As soon as Lakshman left, Ravan took the form of a sadhu. He stood outside the magic circle and asked Sita to give him something to eat as he was very hungry.

Sita stepped out of the magic circle. The sadhu immediately turned into Ravan and carried Sita off in his flying chariot.

Sita cried out for help. Jatayu, King of the Vultures, heard her and attacked Ravan fiercely.

Ravan cut off Jatayu's wings. Jatayu fell to the ground.

Ravan flew with Sita over rivers, forests and mountains to Lanka.

In Lanka, Ravan showed Sita his large palaces and the most beautiful jewellery. He told Sita he was the most powerful King in the world. He asked Sita to marry him.

Sita refused. Ravan flew into a rage. He told the demons to take
Sita to the Ashok Garden and guard her day and night.

Meanwhile Ram and Lakshman were looking for Sita everywhere.
They came upon the dying Jatayu who told them that Ravan had
carried away Sita.

Ram and Lakshman set off in the direction that Jatayu had pointed.

They met a Monkey Prince, Sugreev, who had been driven out of his kingdom by his elder brother, Bali. Ram and Sugreev became friends and promised to help each other. Ram promised to help Sugreev defeat Bali and get back his kingdom and Sugreev promised to help Ram find Sita.

Sugreev went to the palace and challenged Bali to a fight. Bali was stronger than Sugreev. Ram wanted to help Sugreev but could not tell which was Sugreev and which was Bali. Bali defeated Sugreev.

Sugreev was angry with Ram for not helping him. Ram told Sugreev to fight with Bali again.

But this time Sugreev wore a garland of flowers so that Ram could recognise him.
Sugreev and Bali fought again.
Ram shot an arrow and killed Bali.

It was now Sugreev's turn to help Ram. Sugreev sent his army of monkeys and bears to search for Sita. But both Sugreev and Ram thought that Hanuman, the son of Vayu the Wind God, was the most likely to find Sita. Ram gave his ring to Hanuman to show Sita that he had come from Ram.

Hanuman reached the seashore with some of the army.
He took a mighty jump and flew with the speed of the wind towards Lanka.

On the way Hanuman had to face many dangers. There was a sea monster, Surasa, who opened her mouth wide and said, "I want to eat you."

Hanuman made himself as small as a mosquito. He flew into her mouth and then out again very quickly.

When he reached Lanka, Hanuman looked everywhere for Sita. Finally he found her in the Ashok Garden.

When Sita was alone, Hanuman gave her Ram's ring. Sita gave Hanuman one of her jewels for Ram.

To frighten Ravan, Hanuman destroyed trees and plants and killed many demons.

Ravan's son, Indrajit, finally captured Hanuman and took him before Ravan.

Ravan was very angry with Hanuman. He set fire to Hanuman's tail.
Hanuman's tail grew longer and longer.
With his burning tail, Hanuman set fire to Ravan's palaces and buildings.

Hanuman flew back to Ram and gave him the jewel Sita had given him.

Ram, Lakshman, Sugreev and his army set off for Lanka.
They reached the seashore but did not know how to cross the ocean to reach Lanka.

Finally it was decided to build a bridge across the ocean. The army of monkeys and bears began to pull out big trees and roll down large rocks to make the bridge.

Among those helping to make the bridge was a small squirrel. She carried tiny pebbles in her paws and put them with the big trees and large rocks.

The monkeys and bears laughed at her. But Ram lifted up the little squirrel, and stroked her back. The marks of Ram's fingers are still found on the backs of squirrels and remind us of Ram's love for the squirrel who helped him build the bridge to Lanka.

When the bridge was ready, Ram, Lakshman and all the monkeys and bears crossed over to Lanka.

Ram ordered the army to attack. It was a fierce battle between the army of monkeys and bears and the demons. Thousands were killed.

During the battle, Ravan's son, Indrajit, shot magic poisonous snakes at Ram and Lakshman.

The snakes wound themselves around Ram and Lakshman and the two princes could not move.

Then Garuda, the eagle, King of the birds, arrived. The snakes saw Garuda and fled because the eagle kills and eats snakes.

The battle continued. Hundreds and thousands of demons were killed.

Finally, Ravan said, "Wake up my brother Kumbhkaran. He is the mightiest of the demons. He will help us."

Kumbhkaran was as big as a mountain. He slept for six months of the year. He was always very, very hungry when he woke up so Ravan had mountains of food ready for him.

To wake up Kumbhkaran, they shook him. They shouted in his ears. They beat drums. Then they drove a thousand elephants over Kumbhkaran's body.

At last, Kumbhkaran woke up.

After he had eaten his fill, Kumbhkaran marched into battle.

Ram shot one arrow after another at Kumbhkaran and cut off
Kumbhkaran's legs. But Kumbhkaran kept moving forward, fighting.
Then, Ram shot an arrow at Kumbhkaran's head and cut it off.

Finally Ravan himself came to the battlefield. He hurled a spear, bright as the sun, at Lakshman. The spear pierced Lakshman's chest and Lakshman fell to the ground.

Ram was filled with sorrow. But he was told that a special herb, the sanjivini, which grew on the mountain in the Himalaya, would cure Lakshman.

So Hanuman immediately set off for the mountain. But, when he got there, he could not recognise the sanjivini herb. "I will take back the whole mountain," he said, and lifting the entire mountain flew back to the battlefield.

With the sanjivini herb, Lakshman immediately revived and his
wounds healed.

Then Ravan himself came to the battlefield.

Ram faced Ravan. He pierced Ravan's ten heads, one by one, with his arrows. But as one head fell, another grew in its place.

Finally Ram used a special weapon, which flew through the air, giving out flames, and killed Ravan.

Sita was given the news of Ram's victory. She came in a palanquin.
Ram, Sita and Lakshman got into a magical chariot which carried them
through the air to Ayodhya.

Bharat came with Ram's sandals on his head and put them on Ram's feet.

Ram was crowned King.
The city was decorated with flowers and oil lamps were lit at night.
We still celebrate this event on Diwali.

With Ram as King everyone was happy — trees blossomed and had fruit all year round, birds sang and the elephant and the lion lived as friends.